# The Lost Tail

## Gill Scriven

**OXFORD**
UNIVERSITY PRESS

Great Clarendon Street, Oxford OX2 6DP

Oxford University Press is a department of the University of Oxford.
It furthers the University's objective of excellence in research, scholarship,
and education by publishing worldwide in

Oxford  New York
Athens  Auckland  Bangkok  Bogotá  Buenos Aires  Calcutta
Cape Town  Chennai  Dar es Salaam  Delhi  Florence  Hong Kong  Istanbul
Karachi  Kuala Lumpur  Madrid  Melbourne  Mexico City  Mumbai
Nairobi  Paris  São Paulo  Singapore  Taipei  Tokyo  Toronto  Warsaw

and associated companies in  Berlin  Ibadan

Oxford is a trade mark of Oxford University Press
in the UK and in certain other countries

Text © Gill Scriven 2000
First published 2000

All rights reserved. No part of this publication may be reproduced,
stored in a retrieval system, or transmitted, in any form or by any means,
without the prior permission in writing of Oxford University Press,
or as expressly permitted by law, or under terms agreed with the appropriate
reprographics rights organisation. Enquiries concerning reproduction
outside the scope of the above should be sent to the Rights Department,
Oxford University Press, at the address above

You must not circulate this book in any other binding or cover and you must
impose this same condition on any acquiror

British Library Cataloguing in publication Data
Data available

ISBN 0 19 917340 0

Available in Packs
Stage 7–9 Pack (one of each book)    ISBN 0 19 917344 3
Stage 7–9 Class Pack (six of each book)    ISBN 0 19 917345 1

Printed in Hong Kong

In the school hall the chairs were set out.
There was so much talking, you had to shout.
There were aunts and uncles, dads and mums.
Well! A play by Class Two! Everyone comes!

Mrs Brown's class were doing a show,
'Jack and the Beanstalk', a story
you know.
They practised the dances round and
round.
They painted the giant's house, down to
the ground.

The classroom was noisy, Mrs Brown hurried round.
She said, "Please don't leave your clothes on the ground."
Christopher was sleepy, just half awake.
Angela Philpot had stomach ache.
Sophie and Yazmin kept turning around.
Phil lost his cow tail. It could not be found.

"Dear me!" said Mrs Brown. "Where can it be?"
"We must try and find it, come and help me."
Everyone hunted. They gazed at the ground –
under Adam's clothes, left in a great mound, but Phil's lost tail just could not be found.

"Never mind, Phil," Mrs Brown said at last, "The audience is waiting, we shall have to think fast."

Mrs Brown found some string and she tied it round Phil.

"Now all line up. Stand very still."

The hall went quiet as the lights went dim.
Phil's little sister waved at him.
Phil looked at his string tail, trailing on the ground,
and wished that his cow tail could have been found.

The chorus was first on with a song to sing about how Jack was lazy and wouldn't do a thing.
Then on came Adam, who played Jack.
(He had a loud voice, you could hear at the back.)
Sophie was Jack's mother in a white dress. She asked Jack to help. He couldn't care less.

Then Jack's mother said, "Jack, you must go to the town …"

She stopped, her mouth open, and looked at Mrs Brown.

Mrs Brown whispered, "Take our cow …"

"Oh yes," said Jack's mum, "I remember now. Take our cow and sell it for some money. There's nothing to eat but brown bread and honey."

The cow (Phil) and Jack walked round and round.
Jack trod on Phil's tail, trailing on the ground.
In came Christopher. He made a low bow.
He gave Jack magic beans to pay for the cow.

Now Christopher and Phil had to go away and wait at the side till the end of the play. They sat very still. They couldn't make a sound.
Phil twisted his string tail round and round.

Jack's mum made a face, she pretended to be mad.
"Jack," she said, "you're very, very bad!"
She took the magic beans, and threw them on the ground.
"Ow", said Fay. Mrs Brown frowned.
Phil sat waiting, crouched on the ground,
twisting his string tail, round and round,
as up sprang the beanstalk to a tinkling sound.

"Look!" said Jack's mum. "A beanstalk has grown.
It must be where those beans were thrown."
Yasmin was the beanstalk. She waved about, while the clouds did a dance, skipping in and out.

Jack climbed the beanstalk, right to the top.
The beanstalk giggled. Mrs Brown whispered, "Stop!"
Jack went to the giant's house and knocked on the door.
He knocked too quietly, so he knocked some more.
The giant's house wobbled. It nearly fell down.
Class Two giggled and looked at Mrs Brown.

Abdul was the giant. He wore a gold crown. Jane was his wife in a pink dressing gown.
"Come in," said the giant's wife and Jack went inside.
Then along came the giant, and Jack had to hide.

Katie had a xylophone. She made the sound of an enormous giant's footsteps, pounding the ground.

The giant said the words that a giant has to say, "FE FI FO FUM" in a fierce way.

The giant went to sleep … he snored, which was funny.

Jack stole the giant's bag with all the giant's money.

Jack stole the magic hen, and he stole the harp too.

The giant woke up and shouted, "I see you!"

Phil sat waiting, crouching on the ground, twirling his string tail around and around. Jack jumped down the beanstalk in one big bound.

The giant chased after him. He'd nearly reached the ground.
Growling and scowling, he made a dreadful sound.
Jack got an axe. He whirled it in the air.
It was only made of cardboard so the beanstalk didn't care.

The beanstalk waved her arms about then toppled gently down.
The giant toppled after her and squashed his crown.
Jack said, "I'm rich. I've got the giant's money."
Jack's mum was happy. She could buy some more honey!

Michael and Stephen made a trumpet sound.
Class Two came on and gathered all around.
Just time for photographs and one last bow.
Phil's little sister called, "Where's the cow?"
Where was the cow? He had to be found.
"Oh dear, look at Phil, all tangled on the ground."

Mrs Brown rescued him, she said, "Here's our cow!
Phil, take off the cow's head, let's see you now."

Phil took off the cow's head, and something dropped out.
Phil picked it up. You should have heard him shout!

"MY COW TAIL! It's found!
It's here, on the ground!"
Phil gave a low bow.
We all cheered for
the cow.